ex libns

Alan Sinclair 2005
purchased from J. Barnett

Contents

First published 2005

ISBN (10) 0 7110 3033 2
ISBN (13) 978 0 7110 3033 6

All rights reserved. No part of this book may be reproduced or transmitted in any form or by any means, electronic or mechanical, including photocopying, recording or by and information storage and retrieval system, without permission from the Publisher in writing.

© Ian Allan Publishing Ltd 2005

Design by Hieroglyph

Published by Ian Allan Publishing

An imprint of Ian Allan Publishing Ltd, Hersham, Surrey KT12 4RG

Printed by Ian Allan Printing Ltd, Hersham, Surrey KT12 4RG

Code: 0510/B1

Visit the Ian Allan Publishing website at www.ianallanpublishing.com

Front cover: There were still significant independent operators in Scotland and north-east England in 1970, like the Ayrshire co-operatives, of which A1 Service was the biggest. The members invested in new high-capacity buses like this 1968 Leyland Atlantean PDR2/1 with 79-seat Park Royal dual-door bodywork. It was owned by Docherty, Irvine.
Harry Hay

Back cover, upper: A Scottish Bus Group vehicle that would probably have looked more at home in a National Bus Company fleet, a Bristol RELL6G with 53-seat Eastern Coach Works body, one of 12 delivered to Alexander (Fife) in 1968.
Harry Hay

Back cover, lower: Eastern Scottish and United Auto buses shared a bus station and adjacent depots in the border town of Berwick-upon-Tweed. This is a 1961 United Bristol MW5G with 45-seat ECW body, on a local service in Berwick.
Harry Hay

Previous page: The National Bus Company's two territorial operators in north-east England in 1970 were United Auto and Northern General. The Northern group operated under its own name as well as the names and liveries of subsidiaries, usually former tramway companies. The largest of these in 1970 in fleet size was Sunderland District, with 93 buses, including this slightly scruffy 1962 Leyland Atlantean PDR1/1 with ungainly Roe bodywork.
Geoff Lumb

This page: Although Central SMT was not the Scottish Bus Group's largest company, and its operating territory was relatively small, it provided an intensive and profitable service network in Dunbartonshire and Lanarkshire. Leaving Glasgow's newly-opened Anderston bus station is B111, a 1960 Bristol Lodekka LD6G with 60-seat ECW body.
Alan Millar

Facing page: In the mid-1960s several fleets covered by this book had bought dual-door rear-engined single-deckers for driver-only operation. This was particularly true of the municipal operators, and Darlington Corporation no.15 is a 1967 Daimler Roadliner SRC6 with Roe 47-seat bodywork.
Daimler

Introduction

In many ways the year 1970 marked the end of an era for the British bus industry. The bus business had come from the early postwar highs when it couldn't get enough new buses to satisfy the passenger demand, and into a period of steady decline in passenger numbers, growth in private motoring and ever-rising costs, and clearly this couldn't go on. The government stepped in by regrouping many of the major players and introducing Bus Grants as an incentive to operators to invest in new buses suitable for driver-only operation.

So by 1970 the former rival Tilling and BET groups were merged into the new National Bus Company, the first four Passenger Transport Executives had been created, London Country had been hived off from London Transport and placed under NBC ownership, and control of the Scottish Bus Group had returned to Scotland under the new Scottish Transport Group.

Several of these moves affected companies covered in this book. There was little outward sign of the changes in Scotland, except that the David MacBrayne business passed into the hands of the new STG and its bus services were gradually passed on to other SBG companies. In the north-east of England the two big territorial companies, United Auto and Northern General, were now partners in NBC, although corporate liveries and fleetnames were still a couple of years away. And Newcastle and South Shields municipal buses passed to the new Tyneside PTE.

Round the corner were periods of industrial unrest that would seriously affect new bus deliveries in the 1970s, and further away were changes that few in 1970 could have anticipated – notably deregulation and privatisation.

But this is a picture of 1970, and although not all of the photos were taken in 1970, they show what the bus scene was like in that year. My thanks to the photographers who supplied the pictures in this book, and I am particularly pleased to include a number of pictures taken by Harry Hay. Harry was a friend for many years, a well-travelled enthusiast and a professional busman, latterly with the Ayrshire independent, Shuttle Buses. Sadly, Harry died in middle age, but his photos were passed on to the Scottish Branch of The Omnibus Society, which is anxious to share his work with a wider audience.

Gavin Booth
Edinburgh

Scotland and North-East England Snapshot

Over the centuries the border town of Berwick-upon-Tweed has marked the boundary between Scotland and England, although the town itself has been under Scottish and English control at various times. Now firmly established in England, Berwick is a symbol of the close ties that still endure between Scotland and North-East England. Both areas complain of remoteness from London and the Westminster parliament and a feeling that their local situation is not fully understood. When devolution gave the Scots their own parliament in 1999, the people of the north-east may have looked at this with envious eyes, yet moves to devolve more power to the English regions seem to have been rejected.

Back in 1970 in Scotland there was a re-awakening of interest in nationalism, prompted by the election of Winnie Ewing as the Scottish National Party's first MP. In transport this had been reflected in the 1969 creation of the Scottish Transport Group, a state-owned body that assumed control of the 4,700 buses of the Scottish Bus Group, previously owned by the Transport Holding Company, together with the ferry services of the formerly railway-owned Caledonian Steam Packet company and THC's half interest in David MacBrayne Ltd, the shipping, road haulage and bus operator; during 1969 STG acquired the privately-held half interest in MacBrayne, which then became a wholly owned subsidiary.

As a result, control of Scotland's state-owned buses returned to Scotland after 20 years under the London-based British Transport Commission and its successor, the Transport Holding Company. Scottish Bus Group (SBG) was particularly strong in Scotland's most populous areas, with substantial urban networks in towns that lacked their own municipally-owned buses, a widespread network of interurban services, and rural services in areas like the Borders, south-west and north-east Scotland, and the Highlands. The most obvious gap in the SBG map covered the north-west and the islands, where MacBrayne operated, often in conjunction with its shipping services, and there was a long tradition of small local operations. In 1970 SBG had Scotland's biggest bus fleet, operating through its seven subsidiaries plus MacBrayne. The seven SBG operating companies ranged in size from Highland Omnibuses, with just 200 buses, to giants like Scottish Omnibuses with 900 buses, Alexander (Midland) with 950 and Western SMT with 1,020. MacBrayne had 142 buses.

Outside SBG the four municipal operators, Aberdeen, Dundee, Edinburgh and Glasgow, mustered nearly another 2,500 buses, with Glasgow Corporation accounting for half of these. Their operations were largely confined within the city boundaries, often running in parallel with longer-distance SBG services; municipal interests were protected by higher fares where SBG services were permitted to pick up and set down the same passengers within the boundary, as in Edinburgh, or by preventing local passengers from using SBG services, as in Glasgow.

Although in 1970 a substantial proportion of Scotland's buses were in public ownership, there was an important independent sector, often providing essential services in deeply rural areas. The expansion of the SMT Group in the 1930s was partly through acquisition, but there were still pockets where significant independents survived. Some famous names, like Baxter's of Airdrie, Laurie of Hamilton, and Simpson's of Rosehearty had sold out to SBG in the 1960s, but in Ayrshire there were the three co-operatives, AA, A1 and Clyde Coast,

and around Paisley important local services were operated by Cunningham, Graham, McGill, and Paton. Other independents with more substantial fleets included T D Alexander of Arbroath, Garelochhead Coach Services, Hutchison of Overtown, and McLennan of Spittalfield.

Most other independent stage carriage services were provided by smaller companies, often with a small fleet of buses that were operated alongside coaches for hire and excursion work.

Across the border in north-east England, two large territorial operators dominated the scene – United Automobile Services and Northern General Transport. By 1970 they were both fellow companies in the new National Bus Company, but previously they had been part of the state-owned Tilling (United) and privately-owned BET (Northern) groups.

At one stage United's operating territory had stretched from the Scottish border to East Anglia, but since the 1930s its home patch had been smaller, but still stretched from Berwick to North Yorkshire. Following the creation of NBC in 1969, the United outpost at Carlisle had been transferred to fellow NBC company, Ribble. In 1970 United had over 1,000 buses and coaches.

Within United's sprawling area was the concentrated territory of the Northern General group of companies, with over 800 buses running mainly urban and interurban services in what had just become Tyneside Metropolitan County and south into County Durham. Northern General had been set up by BET in 1913 to consolidate its transport interests in the area, and although subsidiary companies still carried historic names and separate liveries, under NBC's corporate livery these differences would quickly disappear – indeed the separate companies would disappear in the mid-1970s.

Tyneside Passenger Transport Executive was the last of the four original PTAs to be set up in 1969/70. It absorbed the Newcastle and South Shields municipal transport undertakings into Tyneside PTE, which adopted a yellow/cream livery, and was in bus fleet terms by far the smallest of the four pioneering PTEs with only 415 buses. The services of the former Newcastle Corporation undertaking represented a substantial part of the PTE's operations until the expansion to include Sunderland in 1974 under the newly-created Tyne & Wear PTE, and the creation of the successful Metro light rail system.

Other municipal operations in the north-east were unaffected by the creation of the PTE. Darlington and Hartlepool continued as before, but in 1968 Middlesbrough and Stockton corporations and the Tees-side Railless Traction Board merged as Teesside Municipal Transport, following the creation of Teesside County Borough, and in 1974 further local government changes led to the setting up of Cleveland Transit. In 1970 Sunderland Corporation was still under municipal control.

As with parts of Scotland, independent bus operators played an important part in the north-east of England. The largest was Venture Transport, though in May 1970 it sold out to Northern General; the Venture name was retained until the mid-1970s.

The main pockets of independent operation were in County Durham, notably in the southern part of the area, around Bishop Auckland and Durham itself. The best-known was probably OK of Bishop Auckland, which would go on to considerable growth before selling out to Go-Ahead, Northern's privatised successor. Other well-known independents included Bond Bros, Diamond Bus Service, Gillett Bros, Gipsy Queen, Lockey, Trimdon, Stanhope and Weardale.

1970
A pivotal year

The bus industry in Britain probably needed the big shake-up that followed the 1968 Transport Act. Passenger figures had been in steady decline for nearly 20 years and many bus companies seemed more anxious to remain financially afloat rather than stem the decline. As passenger numbers fell, costs were rising – and in particular the less controllable costs that represent a large proportion of any bus company's expenditure, fuel prices and staff wages. In the 1950s rising fuel costs were tackled by a move towards lighter buses, and in the 1960s by a move to longer buses with more seats. The staff costs were tackled by the introduction of driver-only operation, first on single-deckers and then on double-deckers after this became legal in 1966.

The Labour government recognised that something had to be done about the bus industry and so major changes were proposed. Remember that much of the industry was in public ownership through the 1960s. There was the municipal sector, with nearly 18,000 buses, and the state-owned fleets that came under the Transport Holding Company with a further 23,000 buses. Under THC was London Transport (8,200 buses), the Tilling Group (9,900 buses) and the Scottish Bus Group (4,900 buses), and the largest privately-owned fleet was the BET Group's 11,000 buses. But in 1967 BET sold its UK bus interests to THC, which paved the way for a truly Britain-wide state-owned bus giant. That

almost happened, but the growth of nationalism in Scotland led to the creation of a separate Scottish body.

So on 1 January 1969 new state-owned bodies assumed control of a large slice of the British bus cake. National Bus Company brought together the Tilling and BET groups and tried to create a common body out of two very different organisations. 'National' in NBC terms was England and Wales; control of the Scottish Bus Group returned to Scotland after a 20-year gap with the creation of the Scottish Transport Group, which controlled SBG as well as the ferry services of the Caledonian Steam Packet and David MacBrayne companies. MacBrayne was of course a substantial bus operator, but its bus services would be absorbed into other SBG operations. Ownership of London Transport changed a year later, on 1 January 1970, when the Greater London Council assumed responsibility for the red Central Area and control of the

The corporate NBC image was still a couple of years away in 1970, and so United Auto still presented the outward appearance of a traditional Tilling Group fleet, with the red/cream livery and a fleet that consisted largely of Bristol chassis with Eastern Coach Works bodies. A 1970 delivery, no.629, is seen at Marlborough Crescent bus station in Newcastle; it is a Bristol VRTSL6G with 70-seat ECW body.
Mark Page

Country Area and Green Line services passed to a new NBC company, London Country Bus Services.

Another major plank of the 1968 Act was the creation of transport authorities in four of England's major conurbations – the West Midlands, south-east Lancashire/north-east Cheshire, Merseyside and Tyneside. The new Passenger Transport Authorities (PTAs) would plan, co-ordinate and organise public transport in their designated areas, while Passenger Transport Executives (PTEs) would run the day-to-day operations. The original PTEs would grow in the 1970s and more would be created, covering Greater Glasgow, South Yorkshire and West Yorkshire; all would absorb the municipal bus operations in their areas and in some cases local NBC operations, and although they had to sell their direct bus operations in the 1990s, the PTEs are still an important force in their local areas.

All of the changes around 1970 were happening in a bus industry that was not only moving towards increasingly centralised control, but was still heavily regulated. Although there was effectively some competition between bus operators where they operated on common corridors, the licensing regime controlled by the Traffic Commissioners ensured that most

routes enjoyed a monopoly, and that this was fiercely protected. Changes could only be made to bus fares with the approval of the appropriate commissioners, and bus operators had to make a good case for fares increases in the face of objections from everyone from other operators, passenger groups and even British Rail.

The new shape of the bus industry that followed the 1968 Act would survive a decade or so before the Conservative government of the 1980s started to dismantle the regulatory system that had been in place for half a century and the ownership structure that dated back more than 30 years when the Tilling and Scottish groups and London Transport passed into state ownership – and indeed back to the late 1920s when the railways took shareholdings in territorial bus companies and to 1933 when the London Passenger Transport Board was created. Another provision in the 1968 Act that would change the face of the bus industry was the introduction of the Bus Grant scheme, which was set up to help bus operators to upgrade their fleets with buses suitable for driver-only operation. These grants, initially for 25% of the cost of new buses meeting certain conditions, rose to 50% before gradual reduction and the closure of the scheme. Bus operators were not slow to take advantage of this government generosity and flocked to order new buses from the UK's bus manufacturers – essentially the giant Leyland group with Bedford, Ford, MCW and Seddon nibbling at the edges. The lack of model choice would cause problems and open the door to manufacturers like DAF, Scania and Volvo to export chassis to the UK, and even to build them here. Leyland's market domination led to dissatisfaction among some major operators who resented what was seen as an arrogant approach to the customer. The message from

Above: Although some independent operators relied heavily on secondhand purchases, others went for new vehicles, like the Lanarkshire operator, Hutchison of Overtown. An AEC Reliance/ Willowbrook 36ft-long service bus leaves the company's garage to go on to service.
R L Wilson

Left: Sunderland Corporation tried a range of rear-engined single-deck models for its flat fare operations, including Bristol RELL6Gs with Metro-Cammell 47-seat bodies built to match earlier Strachans-bodied buses.
G Coxon

The Scottish Bus Group favoured the rear-engined Albion Viking for lighter duties in the three Alexander fleets. Alexander (Northern) NNV85, new in 1970, is a VK43BL model with 40-seat coach-seated body, seen in Grantown-on-Spey when new, on touring work.
Iain MacGregor

SBG companies generally avoided the lower-built rear-engined single-deckers for bus work, preferring the trusted Leyland Leopard with Alexander Y type bodywork. Western KL2188, a 1968 PSU3/3R with 49-seat dual-purpose bodywork is seen at speed on the M6 motorway near Carlisle.
Peter W Robinson

Leyland was interpreted as 'you will take what we choose to build', which many operators resented. The industrial unrest in the early 1970s with short-time working led to massive delays in the delivery of new buses meant that already overstretched factories could not build the buses ordered under the Bus Grant scheme, and chassis and body supply got completely out of step for a while.

But all of this was still to come. In 1970 operators were working hard to come to terms with their new masters and hoping that the massive changes that came from the 1968 Act would give the industry the stability it needed to concentrate on winning back passengers and keeping ever-spiraling costs down.

To the bus passenger and the casual observer in 1970, there was little external indication that ownership of the BET, Tilling and Scottish groups had changed. The buses still looked the same – corporate liveries and fleetnames were at least a couple

of years away – and the routes were still largely as before. In red London bus territory only the legal lettering on the vehicles betrayed the ownership change – London Transport Executive became London Transport Board. In London's Country Area the changes would soon be more obvious as it moved from the London Transport to the National Bus Company culture.

Leyland dominated the bus market in 1970 because it had seen off much of the competition. Although buses designed by and badged as AECs, Bristols, Daimlers and Guys were still nominally available, the imminent Bus Grant scheme had sounded the death-knell for long-running and in some pockets still popular types like the AEC Regent, Bristol Lodekka, Daimler CVG6 and Guy Arab; the last examples of Leyland's own front-engined Titan had been delivered late in 1969. The choice offered by British Leyland – the name adopted after the merger with British Motor Holdings in 1968 that brought

Daimler and Guy into the fold – were the Atlantean, Fleetline and VRT double-deckers, and the Leopard, Panther, LH, RE, Reliance, Swift and Fleetline single-deckers.

The double-deckers, in gradually improved versions, would survive through the 1970s until Leyland came up with an acceptable replacement in the shape of the Olympian. The Leopard survived, increasingly as a coach chassis, but with substantial bus orders from state-owned groups like Scottish Bus and Ulsterbus, and the Reliance was still favoured as a premium coach chassis through the 1970s; the Leopard and Reliance were effectively replaced by Leyland's Tiger. The LH continued as a lighter-weight bus and coach chassis, but while the Bristol RE enjoyed continued sales as an 'export' model to Ulsterbus/Citybus, British operators were unable to buy it, although several wanted to, or the Panther or Swift, which weren't mourned quite so much. The reason these rear-engined bus chassis, introduced only in the 1960s, bit the dust so soon was the Leyland National, the integral single-decker that was introduced to the world in the autumn of 1970 at the Commercial Motor Show.

Firms that would later make an impact in the UK, Volvo in particular, were still waiting in the wings in 1970, and only the Metro-Scania single-decker, a joint venture between Scania and MCW, represented any degree of European influence. Otherwise you could buy a Bedford or Ford chassis for bus work, and many operators went for these lighter-weight chassis, or a Seddon RU, a rear-engined single-decker in the Bristol RE mould. Dennis, which since the 1990s has been such a significant force on the UK bus market, was going through one of its periods when it concentrated on other products.

Operators like to have choice and their dissatisfaction with Leyland's near-monopoly would be aggravated by the industrial unrest of the early 1970s that sometimes led to bus orders being fulfilled years late. This situation opened the gates to European imports and by the end of the 1980s even the once-mighty Leyland had sold out to Volvo, and Bedford, Ford and Seddon had either abandoned bus production or, in the case of Bedford, pulled out of truck and bus production altogether.

So in a host of ways 1970 was a pivotal year for the bus industry in the UK.

Left: The dramatic move towards rear-engined double-deckers during the 1960s meant that many fleets found themselves with batches of front-engined buses that were unsuitable for driver-only operation when this was legalised in 1966. This Dundee Corporation Daimler CVG6 with Weymann 65-seat body was new in 1957 and would survive into the Tayside Regional Council fleet 18 years later. From 1964 Dundee started to buy Daimler Fleetlines.
Harry Hay

Below: The larger territorial companies cross-subsidised many of their more rural services from the takings on their urban and interurban networks, and bought lighter-weight buses to keep costs down. At Hexham is United Auto no.1519, a 1970 Bristol LH6L with ECW 45-seat body, one of a substantial fleet of over 200 LHs bought between 1968 and 1979.
Mark Page

Northern Scotland and the Islands

Although it represents the greatest area covered in this book, Northern Scotland and the islands had the sparsest population density and as a consequence the fewest buses. Defined here as the counties of Aberdeenshire, Argyllshire, Banffshire, Caithness, Inverness-shire, Morayshire, Ross and Cromarty, and Sutherland, plus Orkney and Shetland, this is the Scotland of dramatic sea and mountain views and often bleak treeless landscapes.

The two main centres of population were very different. Aberdeen, the grey-granite city on the North Sea coast, poised to benefit greatly in the North Sea oil boom, and Inverness, 'capital of the Highlands', an ever popular tourist gateway to the north and the west. Draw a line between Aberdeen and Inverness and within that area bounded by the North Sea to the north and east are fertile farmland and busy fishing towns and villages. Solid Scottish towns like Banff, Elgin and Nairn were focal points for bus services, and important fishing ports like Fraserburgh and Peterhead had regular services from Aberdeen as well as town services.

North of Inverness the population thins beyond Dingwall, Tain and Dornoch, before you reach Scotland's northern mainland tip and the towns of Thurso and Wick. To the west are the popular tourist haunts of Fort William, Mallaig and Oban,

and the islands, including Mull and Skye, close to the mainland, and the more distant Outer Hebrides.

Geography and population density have inevitably influenced transport provision in the area and while Scottish Bus Group companies traditionally served the north-east, they had left the more remote areas, including the islands, to independent operators and to David MacBrayne.

SBG's operation in the north and north-west was Highland Omnibuses Ltd, the youngest of SBG's seven companies. It was set up in 1952 to combine two existing businesses, Highland Transport and MacRae & Dick, and to this base was quickly added the Inverness area services of the giant Alexander company. Highland was based in Inverness with principal depots at Dingwall, Dornoch, Nairn, Thurso and Wick, and smaller depots and outstations elsewhere. It will be seen that Highland was essentially a mainland operator, with a clearly defined operating area, but

For many years Highland Omnibuses received the cast-offs from the big SBG fleets in central Scotland. In the 1960s and early 1970s significant numbers of Albion Lowlanders were cascaded from the Central and Western fleets. AL22, a 1963 Lowlander LR1 with Northern Counties 71-seat body, acquired from Central SMT in 1965, heads for Dingwall pursued by a well-loaded Leyland truck.
Harry Hay

that was all to change following the creation of the Scottish Transport Group in 1969, which brought the shipping and bus services of David MacBrayne into the new group.

The MacBrayne name was a famous one, dating back to the 19th century, when the company started providing cargo and passenger shipping services between Glasgow and the Highlands, expanding to cover the Western Isles. Bus services started in 1906, but strictly on the mainland until after World War 2 when acquisitions took MacBrayne buses on to the Western Isles. It soon became clear in 1970 that STG was not going to perpetuate the MacBrayne name and a process of service withdrawals and transfers to other STG companies was started. During 1970 a programme of transfers began, including the Fort William and Skye services, which passed to Highland. The more southerly services, including those on the Kintyre Peninsula, passed to Western SMT. The last MacBrayne services, on Mull and Islay, survived to 1972.

Another consequence of the formation of STG was the transfer of Alexander (Midland)'s Oban services and depot to

Highland; this made sense as Oban was remote from the rest of Midland's operations.

The nature of Highland's operating territory meant that for a number of years it had been at the back of the queue for new vehicles from SBG, relying heavily on buses cascaded from the more profitable SBG fleets in Scotland's central belt. In the 1950s and 1960s it received regular injections of five or six new Alexander-bodied AEC Reliances each year, and these were topped up with 30 Albion Lowlanders from the Central and Western fleets, plus assorted Guys and Leylands as well as 16 fairly new 36ft-long AEC Reliances from Scottish Omnibuses.

In 1964 Highland had received four Ford coaches following the takeover of Stark's, Dunbar, by Scottish Omnibuses, and by 1970 there were 33 Fords in the fleet, some others acquired secondhand, but others bought new. From 1966 Highland started buying new Bedfords and Fords for bus and coach work, and it would standardise on Fords until the late 1970s, when new heavyweight vehicles started to dominate the fleet. Its 1970 fleet totalled 201 buses and coaches.

By contrast, SBG's other fleet in the area, Alexander (Northern), was positively stable. Created out of the Northern Area of the giant Alexander company, Alexander (Northern) was based in Aberdeen with depots stretching from Dundee and Perth in the south to Rosehearty and Peterhead in the north-east, and Buckie, Huntly, Elgin and Macduff north-west of Aberdeen. Northern had gone on the acquisition trail in the 1960s, buying up Strachan's Deeside Omnibus Service, Ballater in 1965, Simpson's of Rosehearty in 1966, Burnett's of Mintlaw in 1967, and Mitchell, Luthermuir in the same year. These augmented Northern's strength in the north-east and introduced some unusual vehicle types into the fleet, some surviving into the 1970s. These included short-lived Fodens from Strachan's, double-deck Leyland Tiger PS1s from Simpson's, AEC Regals and Regents from Burnett's and Leyland Tiger Cubs from Mitchell.

Above: **Still in MacBrayne livery but wearing its new Highland fleetnumber, B55, a 1961 AEC Reliance with Duple Midland 41-seat body acquired by Highland with MacBrayne's Inverness area services in April 1970.**
Michael Dryhurst

Left: **One of Highland's early Ford R192s, T18 with Willowbrook 45-seat bus body, in Inverness bus station on a local service.**
B W Spencer

Above: All three Alexander companies converted some of their Alexander 'Coronation' bodied Leyland Royal Tigers from centre entrance to front entrance in the mid-1960s. The first of the batch, NPC1, new in 1952, is seen at Aberdeen bus station. Rebuilt to centre entrance, it is now preserved.

Iain MacGregor

Below: The Alexander companies got long lives out of many of their buses. 1950-built NRB86, a Leyland Titan PD2/1 with Alexander 53-seat lowbridge body, survived until 1972 and is seen working the Elgin town service.

Iain MacGregor

Above: Arran Transport & Trading was set up in 1967, built around the Lennox businesses on this island in the Firth of Clyde, and by 1973 Arran Transport had absorbed all the smaller local bus operators. At Lochranza in 1969 a selection of Arran Coaches Bedfords await passengers from the Caledonian Steam Packet paddle steamer *Caledonia*. The most prominent Bedford is an ex-Central SMT 1955 SBG model with 38-seat Duple bodywork.

Harry Hay

Below: The origins of what became the Sutherland Transport & Trading company dated back to 1878 when horse-drawn mail routes were operated connecting with the Highland Railway at Lairg. These services continued with motorbuses, and at Lairg in 1969 is NS 4745, a 1961 Bedford J4LZ1 with Duple (Midland) 16-seat body, complete with sizeable mail compartment at the rear.

Harry Hay

Above: A&C McLennan of Spittalfield operated a range of local services in Perthshire using a fairly mixed fleet, including buses carrying bodywork built by the operator. DES 241, a 1950 Leyland Tiger PS1 seen in Blairgowrie in 1969, was acquired in 1960 and carries a newer McLennan 35-seat body.

Harry Hay

Above: T D Alexander, the Sheffield-based independent, started operations in Scotland in 1960, in the Arbroath area. Trading as Greyhound, it grew in the 1960s with a fleet of secondhand vehicles. This former Aberdeen Corporation AEC Regent V/Crossley was new in 1955 and was acquired by Greyhound in 1971.

Mark Page

Above: Like Aberdeen, Dundee Corporation favoured AECs and Daimlers and in fact bought nothing else between 1935 and 1975. This 1953 AEC Regent III with 58-seat Alexander body is at the city centre terminal point at Dock Street among Daimlers, all in the drab green/white livery.

Mark Page

Above: A survivor from an earlier age, this Bedford OB/Duple Vista, ATS 689, was still in use by Fyffe, Dundee for day tours in 1970.

Stewart J Brown

Below: Central SMT received SBG's first Bristol Lodekkas, in 1955, and in 1969 12 of them were transferred to Alexander (Fife). FRD106 is at Kirkcaldy bus station in the company of native Lodekkas. It is an LD6G with 60-seat ECW body.

Edward Shirras

Above: Alexander (Fife) bought Daimler Fleetlines from 1968, and FRF3, new that year with Alexander D type 75-seat body, is seen in Kirkcaldy bus station.
B W Spencer

Below: Barrie's Loch Lomond Coaches operated this Ford R192 with 45-seat Willowbrook body from 1968. It is seen at the Balloch terminus, by Loch Lomond.
B W Spencer

Above: **The Dundee livery became darker after 1970 when the white relief disappeared and a darker green appeared on driver-only buses. In Crichton Street is no.30, one of 10 AEC Reliances with Alexander Y type bodies that gained some notoriety at the time because of union objections. Built in 1964, they were delivered to Dundee in 1965, but soon returned for storage at the Alexander coachworks in Falkirk, before returning to Dundee to be registered and placed in service in 1966.**
Mark Page

Left: Garelochhead Coach Services was based to the north-west of Glasgow and sitting at Helensburgh Central rail station is no.78, a very late model AEC Regent V with 64-seat Northern Counties forward entrance body. The blue/yellow symbol on the station is the logo for the 'blue trains', the electric trains that linked Glasgow with the north and south banks of the Clyde.
Harry Hay

The Lothians and the Borders

Two major bus operators were based in Edinburgh in 1970 – Edinburgh City Transport and Scottish Omnibuses – and between them they provided the majority of services that covered the Lothians and the Borders.

Edinburgh is Scotland's capital city, and it is the focal point for a large part of eastern Scotland, including the Lothians and Borders and, particularly following the opening of the Forth Road Bridge in 1964, Fife.

Edinburgh City Transport's operating area in 1970 was more or less defined by the city boundary. It ran a well-established network of mainly cross-city routes with a fleet of 710 buses and coaches, the vast majority Leyland Titans and, increasingly, Atlanteans.

Edinburgh's city transport network at the time was still recognisably based on the tramway system, initially worked by horse-drawn trams followed, at the end of the 19th century, by

cable trams when the city opted for this slightly eccentric form of traction rather than the new-fangled electric trams. The cable cars had all gone by 1923 after Edinburgh belatedly converted to electric trams and one advantage of this was a relatively young tram fleet that saw the system through to the final tramway withdrawal in 1956.

The other major Edinburgh-based operator was Scottish Omnibuses, by that time using the fleetname Eastern Scottish, but still widely known by its pre-state ownership name of SMT. Eastern Scottish had 901 buses in 1970, and although its largest

Edinburgh Corporation had favoured Leylands since the mid-1950s and standardised on Atlanteans from the mid-1960s. At the top of Leith Street is no.896, a 1967 PDR1/1 with Alexander 74-seat bodywork, operating as a driver-only bus.
Gavin Booth

depot was at New Street, in Edinburgh, the majority of the fleet was housed in depots that ranged from Baillieston, on Glasgow's eastern fringes, to Berwick-upon-Tweed, just over the border with England.

Like its fellow Scottish Bus Group companies, Eastern Scottish operated long trunk routes from and between its main centres, as well as local town service networks and infrequent rural services. Routes from Edinburgh to the north and west reached to Glasgow, serving West Lothian on the way, and to the Falkirk/Stirling areas, jointly with Alexander (Midland) and, since 1964, into Fife, jointly with Alexander (Fife). There were also services across the border to Newcastle, jointly with United Auto. It provided high-frequency services between Edinburgh and Dalkeith and the communities in the Midlothian coalfield area, and in East Lothian it served the more prosperous farming and seaside communities.

In addition to the trunk services, Eastern served the border counties of Peebles-shire, Berwickshire, Selkirkshire and Roxburghshire with rural services and, in important centres like Galashiels and Hawick, town services.

Eastern's fleet was fairly mixed in 1970, with fewer Leylands

than most of its fellow SBG companies. AEC Reliance single-deckers had been favoured between 1958 and 1966, and Bristol double-deckers since 1956; most were Lodekkas, but Eastern had recently received VRTs, which were destined for a short stay before they were exchanged for more Lodekkas from NBC fleets.

Bristol single-deckers were also popular, and there were LSs and MWs dating from the mid-1950s and more recent REs and LHs, and Eastern chose Bedfords rather than Fords for its lighter-weight buses.

In the 1950s and 1960s Scottish Omnibuses had acquired significant independents – Lowland Motorways, Baxter's Bus Service and Stark's Motor Services – and in 1970 there were still former Baxter and Stark vehicles in the fleet, as well as 'pure' Eastern Scottish buses painted in the Baxter and Stark liveries, as a concession to local goodwill.

Unlike the west of Scotland there had never been a strong tradition of independent operation in the Lothians and Borders. Apart from miners' services, in the Lothians the most notable independent was Wiles, Port Seton, with a network of local services to the east of Edinburgh. In the Borders there were small operators like Atkinson of Morebattle, French of Coldingham, Kyle Brothers of Kelso and Nicol of Hawick, providing rural links on an infrequent basis.

Edinburgh City Transport became Lothian Region Transport in 1975 at the time of Scottish regionalisation, and stuck with the traditional madder and white livery with new fleet and legal names. In the deregulated market in 1986 it spread its wings to run beyond the old Edinburgh city boundary into Midlothian, East Lothian and West Lothian, in competition with Eastern Scottish.

Lothian continues in local authority ownership as Lothian Buses plc, the last surviving Scottish municipal fleet and the largest in the UK with around 550 buses.

Eastern Scottish reverted to its roots in 1985 when SBG rationalised its operating companies. It lost its Glasgow area to Central and the new Kelvin company, Linlithgow depot to Midland and its East Lothian and Borders depots to the new Lowland Scottish company. This left a depleted Eastern with depots only in Edinburgh, Dalkeith, Musselburgh, Livingston and Bathgate.

In the SBG privatisation, Eastern went first to a management buy-out, but, like Lowland, was subsequently bought by the rising GRT group, predecessor of today's FirstGroup. First Edinburgh now stretches from the English border right through the Borders and Lothians to Falkirk, Stirling and Balfron. In the old Eastern Scottish area First has concentrated on main corridors, and independents have picked up some trunk and local work, particularly in the Borders.

Above: Wiles of Port Seton was one of the few independents in the Edinburgh area. It favoured the Albion Nimbus for service work, like this ex-Halifax 1963 NS3AN example with Weymann 31-seat bodywork, here on an Omnibus Society tour. Gavin Booth

Left: Eastern Scottish bought 34 Bristol LH6P in 1970 with Alexander 38-seat coach bodies. YA339 is seen at Montrose on an extended tour when new. M A Penn

Left: After standardising on AEC Reliances, Eastern turned to the Leyland Leopard for a few years. This 1969 example, from its first batch, is a PSU3/3R with 49-seat Alexander Y type body, ZH397, and is seen passing through the arch of the old castle wall in Alnwick on the 505 Edinburgh-Newcastle service, run jointly with United Auto.
G Coxon

Below: Eastern's last Bristol Lodekkas were 25 extra-long FLF6G with 76-seat ECW bodies, used on the services between Edinburgh and the Dalkeith area. AA217, new in 1966, is seen in North Bridge, Edinburgh.
John Burnett

Above: To replace its trams Edinburgh Corporation famously bought 300 Leyland Titan PD2/20s with ultra-lightweight Metro-Cammell Orion bodywork. No.442, new in 1954 and seen in Princes Street, would complete 20 years service in Edinburgh.
Gavin Booth

Left: Edinburgh later bought Leyland Titan PD3s with Alexander forward entrance bodies, like no.850 of 1966, a PD3A/2 70-seater, seen here in Fountainbridge.
Gavin Booth

Opposite top: When the vast new Wester Hailes housing development was built in the early 1970s, Edinburgh Corporation was quick to introduce services into the developing area. No.605, a 1962 Leyland Titan PD2A/30 with 66-seat Alexander body, approaches Wester Hailes on the new 30 service in February 1970.
Iain MacGregor

Right: From 1969 Edinburgh bought dual-door buses to speed boarding and alighting in the city centre, and was the last fleet in Scotland to stick with this layout. A 1972 Leyland Atlantean PDR1A/1 with 75-seat Alexander J type body, no.287, in York Place.
Gavin Booth

Above: Scottish Omnibuses traded as Eastern Scottish from the mid-1960s and in the 1960s had acquired two well-known independent operators, Baxter's of Airdrie and Stark's of Dunbar. Although the Baxter's name and livery would continue to be used, some former Baxter's buses were transferred to the Edinburgh area, as were buses ordered by Baxter's before the takeover. BB962 was one, delivered new in 1963 to Eastern Scottish, an AEC Bridgemaster with 70-seat Park Royal bodywork; in 1973 it would pass to Highland Omnibuses.
Harry Hay

Below: Buses from the parent Eastern Scottish fleet were transferred to Victoria depot to work in Baxter's livery, like AA999, a 1968 Bristol Lodekka FLF6G with ECW 70-seat body, that had come to Eastern from United Auto in the 1973 exchange.
Harry Hay

The stories of Alexander (Midland) and Eastern Scottish really belong to other chapters, but Central SMT and Western SMT definitely belong here.

Both were created under these names in 1932 when railway company capital allowed the SMT company to expand dramatically. In 1929 it had acquired the Alexander business, and in 1932 it consolidated its position in south central Scotland.

Central SMT was formed from three substantial companies operating in Lanarkshire and into Dunbartonshire after they passed into SMT control. Never one of the SMT's, later SBG's, 'glamorous' companies, Central provided an intensive network in largely industrial areas, and its no-nonsense approach meant that it was SBG's most profitable company.

Its 606-strong 1970 fleet reflected the no-nonsense approach, consisting largely of Bristol Lodekkas and Leyland Titans, and from 1964 a large fleet of Alexander Y type-bodied Leyland Leopards as it moved away from double-deckers. Central developed a reputation for holding on to some types of double-deckers for only a short time: Albion Lowlanders bought in 1962/3 were soon moved on to SBG's Fife and Highland fleets; Bristol VRTs bought in 1969 were exchanged with NBC Lodekkas; and Daimler Fleetlines bought in 1972 were dispersed throughout SBG.

By 1970 Western SMT had grown to be SBG's biggest fleet, with 1,021 buses. It had started as a BET firm, Scottish General Transport, which was sold to SMT in 1931. There followed a number of other acquisitions in Ayrshire and Renfrewshire, and these, plus Midland Bus Services of Airdrie, under SMT control since 1929, were put together as Western SMT in 1932. There were further acquisitions in the 1930s but Western grew dramatically after World War 2 when it acquired Dunlop of

Top: Until the mid-1960s Central SMT operated a largely double-deck fleet, a mix of Bristols and Leylands. This is no.L600, a 1959 Leyland Titan PD2/30 with Northern Counties lowbridge 59-seat body.
Harry Hay

Above: Although Central's heartland was south of Glasgow, in Lanarkshire, it also ran services on the north bank of the Clyde into Dunbartonshire. L626, a 1960 Leyland Titan PD2/30 with lowbridge Northern Counties body, in pleasant surroundings.
Harry Hay

Central's fleet of Bristol Lodekkas included the only examples of the short forward entrance FSF model delivered new to an SBG fleet. B170, a 1963 FSF6G 60-seater, at Airdrie alongside a Western SMT Albion Lowlander and Eastern Scottish vehicles.
Harry Hay

Greenock and Rothesay Tramways, followed, under British Transport Commission ownership of SMT, by the Tilling Group's Caledonian company and the Paisley-based Young's and Paisley & District businesses. Caledonian gave Western a stronghold in the south-west of Scotland, and with Young's and P&D added 270 buses to the fleet in 1950/1.

Although Western's fleet was always broadly in line with SBG standards, it had pronounced views about what it needed, and never seriously pursued the possibility of using lighter buses like Leyland Tiger Cubs, Albion Vikings or the newer Bedfords or Fords. The fleet essentially had either Gardner or Leyland engines, the former fitted to Guy Arab and Bristol single-deckers, and Bristol, Daimler and Guy double-deckers, the latter to Leyland Titans, Albion Lowlanders and Leyland Leopards.

In 1970 the Western double-deck fleet was largely made up of Bristol Lodekkas and Leyland Titans of different types and lengths. Albion Lowlanders were bought in 1962-5, but, like Central's, many were cascaded to the Fife and Highland fleets. Daimler Fleetlines were bought from 1965 and this became the company's standard double-deck model.

Older single-deckers were Bristol MW6Gs and Guy Arab LUFs, and from 1963 the 36ft Leyland Leopard became the standard single-decker, with some Bristol RELH6Gs for the Glasgow-London service in 1966 and the 12m-long REMH6G in 1969. Western received Bristol VRT double-deckers in 1969/70, but by 1974 these had been withdrawn, most finding their way to NBC fleets in the famous exchange for Bristol Lodekkas. Leopards and Fleetlines continued to be the staple diet, and during the 1970s variety appeared in the shape of the Seddon Pennine VII – Gardner-engined, of course – and the Volvo B58 and Ailsa.

Many of Scotland's best-remembered independent operators were based in the south-western area of Scotland, and in 1970 you could still find them in pockets like Ayrshire, Lanarkshire and Renfrewshire.

The Paisley area independents were still active: Cunningham's of Paisley, Graham's of Hawkhead, McGill's of Barrhead, and Paton of Renfrew. Further south were the important Ayrshire co-operatives, formed to fend off competition from Western's predecessor, Scottish General Transport: AA Motor Services of Ayr served the Ayr-Irvine-Ardrossan areas; A1 Service of Ardrossan served the Ardrossan-Kilmarnock corridor; and Clyde Coast of Ardrossan ran north to Largs.

In the Lanarkshire area the largest independent was Hutchison's of Overtown, with services in the Wishaw and Larkhall area, and others included Stokes of Carstairs and Wilson of Carnwath.

Dumfries was another centre for independents, like Carruthers of New Abbey and Gibson of Moffat.

The ownership of the buses in this area has changed dramatically since 1970. As mentioned, Glasgow Corporation has become First Glasgow, which also encompasses much of what remained of Central SMT. In the 1985 SBG reorganisation, two new companies were created in the Glasgow area. Central's

Dunbartonshire area along with Eastern's and Midland's Glasgow area services were combined to create Kelvin Scottish, leaving Central to concentrate on Lanarkshire, Eastern on the Lothians and Midland on its Central Scotland heartland. Further reshuffling combined Kelvin with Central, but industrial troubles weakened the company and led to its sale to Grampian.

Western's huge area, stretching from the Clyde to the Solway, was also split in 1985, creating Clydeside Scottish to concentrate on the northern part of the operation. Again there was reshuffling before the Clydeside part ended up as Arriva Scotland West and the remainder passed to Stagecoach.

The independent operators didn't last too long, either. Most sold out to the big operators, although Hutchison is a notable survivor, having coped with the trauma of deregulation and strengthened its position while the once-strong Central collapsed around it.

Above: **From 1964 Central bought increasing quantities of Leyland Leopards with 53-seat Alexander Y type bus bodies to replace its older lowbridge double-deckers. T68 is a 1968 PSU3/1R model.**
Harry Hay

Left: **Western SMT stuck largely to Gardner and Leyland engines in its buses, and avoided the lighter-weight types favoured by some of its fellow SBG fleets. JB1946 – the J signifying Johnstone depot, the B a Bristol double-decker – is a 1964 Lodekka FLF6G with 68-seat ECW body.**
Harry Hay

Above: Bowling along into Ardrossan on a Workers service, Western no.ND1538, a 1959 Leyland Titan PD3/2 with 67-seat Alexander lowbridge body. At the time, April 1970, the fare on Western's Glasgow-London coach service was £3 single.
Harry Hay

Below: At Renfrew Ferry terminus, in the company of two East Lancs-bodied Leyland Titan PD2s bought by Paton, Renfrew from St Helens Corporation, is Western SMT no.ID1665, a 1961 Leyland Titan PD3A/3 with 67-seat Alexander lowbridge body. It advertises a £3.37½p Glasgow-Manchester return coach fare.
Harry Hay

Above: A locally-built Hillman Imp gives way to a 1960 Western Leyland Titan PD3/3 at a roundabout in Saltcoats. Although the lowbridge bodywork looks like a Northern Counties product, it was in fact built by Burlingham at Blackpool.

Harry Hay

Below: Western's operating territory stretched right down into south-west Scotland and at Whithorn en route for Stranraer is DL1893, a 1964 Leyland Leopard PSU3/3R with Alexander 49-seat dual-purpose body.

Mark Page

Above: **Western started buying Daimler Fleetlines in 1965 and this is JR2152, a 1967 CRG6LX with Northern Counties 75-seat body, at Paisley Cross.**
Harry Hay

Below: **For many years Cunningham, Paisley, relied entirely on secondhand double-deckers for its Renfrew Ferry-Paisley route, run jointly with Paton, Renfrew. Turning at Renfrew Ferry in 1970 with the River Clyde in the background is JCH 260, an ex-Trent 1956 Leyland Titan PD2/12 with Metro-Cammell 59-seat body.**
Harry Hay

Above: A unique vehicle in the fleet of Graham, Hawkhead, was this Guy Arab IV with 69-seat Strachans body, exhibited at the Commercial Motor Show in 1962 and bought by Graham in 1964.
Harry Hay

Below: The smart fleet of McGill, Barrhead, operated from its hometown into Paisley and Renfrew. This is one of two Daimler CVG6 with Massey 61-seat bodies bought new in 1959, seen at St James, Paisley.
Harry Hay

Above: Looking particularly smart, Paton, Renfrew no.1, a 1956 Leyland Titan PD2/20 with Weymann 61-seat bodywork recently acquired from St Helens Corporation, at work on Renfrew Road on the main Paton route between Paisley and Renfrew Ferry.
Harry Hay

Left: The three Ayrshire co-operatives that survived in 1970 had all sprung out of attempts in the 1920s to compete with the BET's Scottish General company, predecessor of Western SMT. Some 40 independents were competing on the Kilmarnock-Ardrossan corridor, among themselves and with Scottish General. They set up Ayrshire Bus Owners in 1926, operating as 'A1' and in 1970 there were still 16 owners. Although many secondhand buses had been operated, A1 owners were expected to invest in new buses, like this Leyland Titan PD2A/30 with 64-seat forward entrance Northern Counties body. There were four of these buses bought by A1 owners in 1962; TCS 105 was owned by J J Stewart, Saltcoats.
Harry Hay

Northumberland

Until the local government reform of 1974 acknowledged the importance of the conurbation defined by Newcastle-upon-Tyne, Gateshead and Sunderland with the creation of Tyne & Wear Metropolitan County, the River Tyne formed Northumberland's southern boundary, the border with Scotland its northern one. Between the two is some of England's most attractive and unspoiled territory, with the Cheviot Hills, Kielder Forest and Hadrian's Wall to the west and the dramatic North Sea coastline to the east. Running south through the county like a spine is the A1 road, which now bypasses important historic towns like Alnwick and Morpeth, and on the other roads heading north and west are towns like Wooler and Hexham. As you get closer to Newcastle the population density increases with important coastal towns like Blyth, Whitley Bay, Tynemouth and North Shields.

For much of Northumberland, United Automobile Services was the principal bus company. Born in 1912 in Suffolk, after World War 1 it expanded north with services in Northumberland and County Durham as well as Lincolnshire and Yorkshire. Tilling & BAT and the London & North Eastern Railway bought a controlling interest in 1929 and United inherited LNER interests in other bus companies in the north-east as well as the railway's own bus services.

In the 1930s the Lincolnshire and East Anglian interests were passed on to the Lincolnshire Road Car and Eastern Counties bus companies and United concentrated on the north-east, with its headquarters at Darlington.

United's main services in Northumberland covered the areas to the north and west with services linking Newcastle with places like Warkworth, Bamburgh and Hexham, and important shorter services to Ashington and Blyth. Some of the main United trunk services were joint with Scottish Omnibuses, linking Newcastle and Edinburgh via Alnwick and Berwick on the A1, Wooler and Kelso on the A697, and Otterburn and Jedburgh on the A68. With end-to-end timings of over five hours, these services were designed mainly for point-to-point traffic and would carry many and varied busloads in the course of their long journeys.

United Auto operated express coach services from Newcastle and other points in the north-east to London. These used smartly-presented coaches in olive green/cream livery, like no.1285, a 1970 Bristol RELH6G with 43-seat ECW body, seen outside Victoria Coach Station in London.
Photobus

The 1970 United fleet of 1,082 buses and coaches comprised 302 double-deckers, 632 single-deck buses and 148 single-deck coaches. The vast majority were Tilling-standard Bristol chassis with ECW bodywork, including LS, MW, SUL and RE single-deckers, and K, KSW, LD, FS, FSF and FLF double-deckers. United had its distinct coach fleet, painted olive green and cream, for prestige services like the Newcastle-London service and its share of the Tyne-Tees-Mersey services linking the north-east with Leeds, Manchester and Liverpool. Non-standard types were AEC and Leyland single-deckers acquired in 1967 with the business of Wilkinson's of Sedgefield.

During 1970 United continued to take delivery of standard Bristol/ECW types – 50-seat dual-purpose RELL6Gs, 49-seat RELL6G buses, 45-seat LH6L buses, 43-seat RELH6G coaches and 70-seat VRTSL6G double-deckers. A new variant was introduced into the fleet with a small batch of 45-seat two-door RELL6G buses, and five Plaxton-bodied LH6L coaches also arrived.

As NBC influence took hold, United's new deliveries in the 1970s would mirror those of many of its NBC brothers – Bristol LHs and VRTs, Leyland Nationals and Leyland Leopard coaches.

Top: United Auto's 1970 fleet was largely made up of standard Tilling-issue Eastern Coach Works-bodied Bristols. This is a 1969 delivery, a 45-seat Bristol LH6L, a type that was used for lighter duties, often replacing Bristol LS types. No.1515 is seen at Berwick-upon-Tweed, at the northern end of United's sizeable operating area, working as a driver-only bus.
Harry Hay

Centre: The prototype Bristol RE bus was used by United Auto, which went on to become an enthusiastic customer for the type in bus, dual-purpose and coach form. Among the 1970 delivery of 54 RE variants were 10 RELL6Gs with 50-seat ECW dual-purpose bodies in this livery style. No.4221 is at Marlborough Crescent bus station in Newcastle.
Mark Page

Left: Another 1970-delivered Bristol RELL6G for United, and although no.4223 is a dual-purpose 50-seater with semi-coach seats, it wears bus livery as it proceeds to Newcastle's Worswick Street bus station, followed by one of Northern's Routemasters.
Charles Dean/Kevin Lane collection

Northern General had a small presence in Northumberland through its Tynemouth and Tyneside subsidiaries. Tynemouth & District had started as a tramway company in the late 19th century operating in the area to the east of Newcastle, taking in Wallsend, North Shields, Tynemouth and Whitley Bay, later expanding to Blyth with motorbuses. Services between Newcastle and Tynemouth/Whitley Bay were operated jointly with United. The Newcastle-Wallsend-North Shields corridor was served by the Tyneside Omnibus company, the 1965 renaming of the 1901-founded Tyneside Tramways & Tramroads company. The Tynemouth and Tyneside fleets were mainly Leyland Titans and Atlanteans, and Tynemouth also operated Daimler Fleetlines.

Until 1 January 1970 the major operator in Newcastle had been, of course, Newcastle Corporation Transport, but from that date it was absorbed into the new Tyneside PTE. With around 400 buses it represented the major part of the PTE; initially South Shields Corporation was the only other municipal undertaking transferred to the PTE. The Newcastle municipal undertaking was regarded as the PTE's Northern Division, and the South Shields undertaking is covered under County Durham, the Southern Division. The Sunderland Corporation bus undertaking was transferred to the PTE in 1973 prior to the creation of the enlarged Tyne & Wear PTE.

Newcastle Corporation had operated electric trams, from 1901-50, then motorbuses, from 1912, and trolleybuses, from 1935-66. Its early motorbuses stretched beyond the tram tracks to places beyond the city boundaries, but gradually replaced the trams and trolleys to provide a city-wide coverage that included services across the Tyne into Gateshead, in conjunction with Northern's Gateshead & District company.

Top: An older United single-deck bus still in service in the southern part of the company's territory is no.2239, a 1957 Bristol LS5G with 45-seat ECW body.
Charles Dean/Kevin Lane collection

Above: The shorter-length forward entrance Bristol Lodekka FSF6B model was bought by United in 1960/1 when 28 were bought. No.264 is from the 1960 batch and like the other FSFs had a 60-seat ECW body.
Charles Dean/Kevin Lane collection

Left:
For many years Northern General's small Tyneside fleet consisted entirely of Leyland double-deckers. Generations of Titans were followed in the mid-1960s by Atlanteans, and this 1966 delivery is a PDR1/1 model with 77-seat Alexander bodywork, seen at Newcastle Central station.
Mark Page

Since 1960 Newcastle had standardised on the Leyland Atlantean for its largely double-deck fleet. It had been an early Atlantean customer and had well over 200 examples bodied by Alexander, Metro-Cammell and Weymann. The most recent examples, delivered since 1966, were two-door buses, and the 1969/70 deliveries were of the 33ft-long PDR2/1R model; the PTE went on to buy large batches of long Atlanteans. Although single-deckers would play a greater part in the PTE fleet, Newcastle Corporation concentrated on double-deckers, though in 1967-9, like many other city operators, it had bought small batches of rear-engined two-door buses; Newcastle's were Alexander-bodied Leyland Panthers.

During 1970 Tyneside PTE took delivery of more 33ft Alexander-bodied Atlanteans that had been ordered by Newcastle Corporation, and placed an order for 25 more. The Atlantean would continue to be king during the 1970s, though with Fleetline deliveries for its South Shields and Sunderland fleets, and substantial orders for 140 Scania-MCW Metropolitans.

Independent bus operators in Northumberland were generally long-established local firms like Bedlington & District, Craiggs of Amble, Hunter of Seaton Delaval, Rochester & Marshall of Great Whittington, Terrier of Choppington, and Tyne Valley of Acomb.

United Auto was subdivided prior to the National Bus Company privatisation, and the section of the operation north of the Tyne, Northumbria Motor Services, was sold to its management in 1987; the United services south of the Tyne went to Caldaire Holdings, apart from Pickering and Scarborough operations earlier transferred to the East Yorkshire company.

Top: Although it had traditionally been a double-deck fleet, Newcastle Corporation bought dual-door Leyland Panthers with Alexander W type bodies in 1967-69. One of its first two, no.502 of 1967, a PSUR1/1 model, is seen when new, passing a Weymann-bodied Leyland Atlantean.
John Burnett

Above: United received its first rear-engined double-deckers in 1969, 20 Bristol VRTSL6Gs with 70-seat ECW bodies. No.619 at Morpeth displaying a staff driver recruitment poster on the side.
Geoff Lumb

After a series of ownership changes, much of the old United Auto company is now back together as Arriva North East.

Tyne & Wear PTE's bus operations were sold in a management/employee buyout in 1994, becoming Busways Travel Services; Busways in turn was sold to Stagecoach.

The Bristol Lodekka was United's standard double-deck model from 1954 to 1968. This is one of its last deliveries, no.560, a 1968 FLF6G with 70-seat ECW forward entrance bodywork. From 1951 until 1969 United had used an alphanumeric numbering scheme which described the chassis and engine type, and in some cases the body type. Early Lodekkas were BL types, but with a fleet consisting entirely of Bristol types, the letter B denoting the chassis type was dropped in 1964. New as L260, the bus shown became no.560 in the 1969 renumbering, which was based purely on numbers. This bus moved north to Western SMT in 1973 when Scottish Bus Group received Lodekkas in exchange for its unloved Bristol VRTs.
Geoff Lumb

Left: The acquisition of the business of Wilkinsons of Sedgefield in 1967 introduced new types into the highly standardised United fleet, mostly AECs and Leylands. Seen as United no.W3, this AEC Reliance MU3RV with Plaxton Highway 45-seat bus body was new to Wilkinsons in 1958.
Geoff Lumb

Below: Leyland Atlanteans also figured in the Tynemouth & District fleet. This is a 1962 PDR1/1 example with 78-seat Metro-Cammell bodywork.
Charles Dean/Kevin Lane collection

Top: Tynemouth & District introduced the Daimler Fleetline into the Northern General fleets. This is one of 10 CRG6LX examples with Weymann 77-seat bodies delivered in 1963. No.270 is at Newcastle Central on private hire work – though hopefully not proceeding as far as Braemar.
Mark Page

Above: Older Leylands in the Tynemouth & District fleet in 1970 were 30ft-long Leyland Titan PD3/4s with Metro-Cammell Orion 73-seat bodies.
Charles Dean/Kevin Lane collection

Tyneside PTE adopted the distinctive yellow/cream livery of its largest constituent, Newcastle Corporation. It had been an early customer for the rear-engined Leyland Atlantean and this 1961 PDR1/1 model, with Alexander 78-seat bodywork, is seen in central Newcastle.
Charles Dean/Kevin Lane collection

Metro-Cammell and Alexander had supplied bodies to Newcastle Corporation on Leyland Atlantean chassis, including some Metro-Cammell versions that carried fronts that matched Alexander deliveries, as on no.130, a 1966 78-seat PDR1/1.
Charles Dean/Kevin Lane collection

Rochester & Marshall of Great Whittington, north of Hexham, was a long-established Northumberland independent, and in 1970 operated a fleet of 15 vehicles on stage carriage services, excursions and tours. This Bedford C5Z1 with Duple Super Vista body is seen at Hexham.
Mark Page

Above: Among the older buses inherited by Tyneside PTE from Newcastle Corporation were Park Royal-bodied AEC Regents dating from 1956/7. No.470, a 1956 62-seater, is seen at Haymarket, Newcastle.

Charles Dean/Kevin Lane collection

Below: Tyne Valley Coaches of Acomb, near Hexham, had a fleet of 24 vehicles in 1970, mostly Bedfords like this Duple-bodied SB5 in the company's Acomb yard.

Mark Page

Durham and Teesside

In 1970 the River Tyne formed the boundary between Northumberland and County Durham. Stretching south to the North Riding of Yorkshire, County Durham's population grew by some 80% in the later part of the 19th century as a result of the coal and iron mining, engineering and railway industries that thrived in the area.

The major population centres in the county were the historic cathedral city of Durham, the ports of Hartlepool and Sunderland, the pioneering railway town of Darlington, and important local centres like Bishop Auckland and Chester-le-Street. Gateshead, considered today in the same breath as Newcastle, was always an important centre, but, like Salford to Manchester, it tended to live in the shadow of its bigger and

better-known neighbour. There were also the New Towns of Newton Aycliffe, Peterlee and Washington that allowed people to move out of sub-standard housing in traditional industrial areas, and the excellent road system encouraged a more flexible workforce and attracted new industries into the area.

For bus operators, the combination of a high population density, a good road system and relatively low car ownership meant that this was good bus territory. The Northern General group was the main beneficiary, but United Auto had a presence, and there were several municipal operators and a clutch of independents.

This was Northern General's heartland, with its headquarters at Bensham, Gateshead; it still operated through subsidiaries

like Gateshead & District and Sunderland District, in addition to the main Northern fleet.

The British Electric Traction company (BET) had set up Northern General Transport in 1913 to consolidate its interests in the area, which were the Gateshead, Jarrow and Tynemouth tramway companies. The Gateshead company had started a motorbus service between Low Fell and Chester-le-Street, then between Chester-le-Street and Durham, and Northern took these over in 1914 to lay the foundations of a significant bus operation.

The Jarrow trams were replaced by buses in 1929, the Tynemouth trams in 1931 and

Above: Northern General went on to receive some very Tilling-style buses, including Bristol RELL6Gs with two-door ECW 44-seat bodies. No.2732, delivered early in 1971, is seen when new.
G Coxon

Left: Northern's staple single-deck purchase through much of the 1960s was the Leyland Leopard with BET-style 53-seat bodywork, typically built by Marshall, although this 1965 example has a 49-seat dual-purpose Weymann body.
Photobus

the Gateshead trams lasted until 1951, BET's last. In 1931 Northern acquired the Sunderland District Omnibus company, and in 1936 the Wallsend-based Tyneside Tramways & Tramroads company.

The separate identities were retained right into the National Bus Company era. Northern's buses were red/cream, as were Tynemouth & District's; Gateshead & District and Tyneside Omnibus were green/cream; Sunderland District was dark blue/white. Another red/cream fleet was Wakefield's Motors, acquired in 1929 and under the control of the Tynemouth company; latterly Wakefield's operated single-deck coaches and double-deck buses, and was absorbed fully by Tynemouth & District at the end of 1969.

The Northern General group had a long history of engineering innovation, including the side-engined single-deckers built in the 1930s and the short-bonnet 38-seaters built for the company before and after World War 2. The 1970 fleet reflected Northern's fondness for AEC and Leyland single-deckers, and Leyland double-deckers – not forgetting the 50 Leyland-engined Routemasters it bought in 1964/5. There were also examples of Leyland's rear-engined Panther, bought in 1968/9.

Northern missed out on new buses in 1970, other than a Plaxton coach-bodied Leopard, and received decidedly non-

Left: Crossing Newcastle's iconic Tyne Bridge, a Northern General Leyland Atlantean PDR1/1 with rather square-rigged Roe 77-seat bodywork, one of a batch of 35 bought in 1962.
Mark Page

Below: Northern General bought 36ft AEC Reliance and Leyland Leopard service buses in the 1960s. This is a Leopard PSU3/2 new in 1967 with Marshall 53-seat body, leaving Newcastle's Marlborough Street bus station.
Mark Page

standard secondhand double-deckers in the shape of former Crosville Bristol Lodekkas. In the next few years Northern would receive new Tilling-style buses in the shape of Bristol RELLs, RELHs and VRTs, and would be an early customer for NBC-standard-issue Leyland Nationals, but it also held on to its BET individuality with deliveries of double-deck and single-deck Daimler Fleetlines as well as substantial Atlantean deliveries.

During 1970 Northern acquired the famous Venture Transport business, the largest independent in the Northern Traffic Area, based at Consett in the north-west of County Durham. The yellow/maroon/cream single-deck fleet had latterly been standardised on Alexander-bodied Leyland Leopards. The 1970 fleet stood at 83 vehicles, and Northern retained the Venture name and livery until 1975.

The Northern General fleet in 1970 totalled some 850 buses, excluding the Venture contribution, just under a half being double-deckers. The individual fleet totals were Northern 581, Gateshead & District 68, Sunderland District 93, Tynemouth & District 89, and Tyneside Omnibus 17.

In 1970 there were three municipal operators in County Durham. The biggest and most northerly was Sunderland Corporation, which had started operating electric trams in 1900 and only bought motorbuses in the late 1920s. As the town grew, so the motorbus fleet grew, while the tramway fleet and system

Above: Wearing a version of Northern's livery with less cream relief, 1961 Leyland Atlantean PDR1/1 with Roe 77-seat body, no.1962 at Sunderland's Park Lane bus station.
Charles Dean/Kevin Lane collection

Left: Northern General's forward entrance Routemasters gave good service on longer-distance routes south from Newcastle. Crossing the Tyne Bridge is no.2124 from the second batch, built in 1965. Like the Gateshead & District Leyland Atlantean that is following, it carries the 'Shop at Binns' adverts that were so characteristic of many buses in the north-east of England.
Gavin Booth

was modernised. Like so many municipal operators, Sunderland decided to abandon trams in favour of buses in the post-World War 2 years, and the final withdrawal was in 1954. In the 1960s a controversial flat-fare token system was introduced along with two-door rear-engined single-deckers of various types, but this was later abandoned.

Traditionally Sunderland Corporation had operated Daimler and Guy double-deckers, and in the 1960s bought Daimler Fleetlines with bodywork to its own design, along with the rear-engined single-deckers, again carrying distinctive bodywork. More than half of the 1970 fleet of 180 buses was single-deck, reflecting the change in vehicle-buying policy.

In 1973 Sunderland Corporation transferred its transport undertaking to Tyneside PTE, in advance of the creation of Tyne & Wear Metropolitan County.

In 1970 another County Durham municipality had been absorbed into the new Tyneside PTE. South Shields operated electric trams from 1906, and replaced these with trolleybuses between 1936 and 1946, the last of which survived until 1964. Like Sunderland, Daimlers and Guys were favoured, as was Roe bodywork. The most recent deliveries to the fleet of around 90 buses had been Daimler Fleetlines and Bristol RESL6Ls with ECW two-door bodies, which passed to the PTE along with front-engined Daimlers. A batch of single-deck Daimler Fleetlines with Marshall two-door bodies that had been ordered by South Shields were delivered to the PTE in 1971.

Municipal transport in Hartlepool had an unusual history. The adjacent but separate boroughs of Hartlepool and West Hartlepool were served by privately-owned electric tramways and in 1924 West Hartlepool started trolleybus operations. When the trams were withdrawn in 1927 Hartlepool become involved in a joint management committee, but when the trolleybuses were withdrawn in 1953 the two boroughs went their separate ways. Hartlepool Corporation's four-bus fleet was operated by the local coach operator, Bee Line, while West

Above: Northern also kept a fleet of coaches like this 1966 Leyland Leopard PSU3/3R with Plaxton Panorama 44-seat body, seen in Stockton High Street.
Photobus

Left: After its rather square Roe and Weymann-bodied Leyland Atlanteans Northern turned to Alexander for its more rounded designs. This 1966 PDR1/1 77-seater is in Durham.
Photobus

Left: In April 1970 the Northern Branch of The Omnibus Society used this Venture Transport 1963 Leyland Leopard/Alexander Y type for a farewell tour before the company was sold to Northern General. It is seen near Blanchland.
G E Hutchinson

Below: Sunderland Corporation's attempts to break away from the bland body styles offered on early rear-engined double-deckers resulted in this design, with front and rear peaked domed and a one-piece flat windscreen. Daimler Fleetline CRG6LW/Roe 77-seater no.287 of 1966 is seen when new, complete with the 'Shop at Binns' advert that could be found on many buses in the north-east.
G Coxon

Hartlepool continued to buy motorbuses for its own use, which it had done since 1920. The two fleets were merged in 1967 to become Hartlepool County Borough Transport Department. The 75-strong fleet in 1970 was split almost exactly between single-deckers and double-deckers, as Leyland Leopards were introduced from the mid-1960s, followed by a substantial fleet of two-door ECW-bodied Bristol RELL6Ls. The bus operation was bought by its employees in 1993, but passed to Stagecoach the following year.

The remaining municipal operation in 1970 was at Darlington, where the corporation operated electric trams from 1904, which were replaced by trolleybuses in 1926. Unusually, Darlington did not operate motorbuses until 1950, and these replaced the trolleybuses between 1951 and 1957. Like South Shields and Sunderland, Darlington favoured Daimlers and Guys with Roe bodywork, and from 1967 switched to two-door Daimler single-

deckers, initially Roadliners, which were followed by Fleetlines (including 12 Marshall-bodied examples in 1970) and these would be followed by Seddon RUs in the 1970s. Darlington was a target for post-deregulation competition, and the municipal company went into administrative receivership and its services were taken over by Stagecoach, which had already established a presence in the town.

County Durham was a hotbed of independent activity, with some north of Durham (including Armstrong, Ebchester; Diamond, Stanley; Economic, Whitburn; General, Chester-le-Street; Gypsy Queen, Langley Park; Jolly, South Hilton), others south of Durham (including Gillett Bros, Quarrington Hill; GNE, Darlington; Scarlet Band, Cornforth; Shaw, Byers Green; Trimdon Motor Services),

some to the west of the county (including Barnard Castle Coaches, Stanhope Motor Services and Weardale Motor Services) and of course the Bishop Auckland area independents (including Bond Brothers, Lockeys and OK Motor Services).

Two of the local independents would be taken over by United Auto in 1974/5 – Gillett Bros and Shaw Bros – and in 1975 Tyne & Wear PTE acquired two Whitburn-based businesses, Anderson and Wilson, who traded as Economic Bus Service. The Economic name continued in use for some years.

Although Teesside was strictly in the North Riding of Yorkshire until 1974, the municipal bus operations have usually been seen as part of the north-east rather than the great county of Yorkshire.

By 1970 the municipal bus operations in the area were under the control of Teesside Municipal Transport, which brought together the borough of Stockton-on-Tees, the urban district

council of Eston and the county borough of Middlesbrough. Stockton had previously been in County Durham.

Stockton and Middlesbrough had previously run trams and motorbuses, and the other component was the Tees-side Railless Traction Board, which was jointly owned by Eston and Middlesbrough.

Stockton and Middlesbrough got involved in municipal transport in 1921 when, with Thornaby, they jointly bought the local company-owned tramway. Stockton and Thornaby operated jointly until Thornaby sold its interest to Stockton and the trams were replaced by buses. Middlesbrough operated trams until 1934.

Middlesbrough and Eston UDC formed a joint board to operate trolleybuses from 1919 as the Tees-side Railless Traction Board, and from 1924 bought motorbuses as well. It was an early trolleybus operator and the second last UK system to close, in 1971.

The three undertakings that were brought together as Teesside Municipal Transport in 1968, Stockton and Middlesbrough corporations and the TRTB, had very different vehicle buying policies. Stockton favoured

Top: Northern's Gateshead & District company operated almost like a municipality in Gateshead and across the Tyne into Newcastle with intensive services. In the 1960s it had replaced its previous brown livery with this green/cream scheme. No.122, an Alexander-bodied Leyland Atlantean PDR1/1 new in 1964 in Gateshead town centre.
Mark Page

Centre: In the distinctive dark blue/white of Sunderland District, a 1969 Leyland Atlantean PDR1A/1 with Alexander 77-seat body, at Bishop Auckland.
Mark Page

Left: In the January 1971 snows, Sunderland District no.280, a 1955 Leyland Tiger Cub PSUC1/1 with Weymann 44-seat bus body demonstrates the stylish fleetnames and high-mounted legal lettering adopted by the Northern General group in the 1960s.
Charles Dean/Kevin Lane collection

After takeover, the Venture name was continued for a short time, with maroon added to the yellow/cream. Ordered by Venture Transport but delivered in 1971, after Northern took over, no.292 in Newcastle.
Mark Page

Ten years separate these two Sunderland Corporation buses. On the left is no.225, a 1958 Daimler CVG5 with 64-seat Roe bodywork, from the period when Sunderland bought several batches of Roe-bodied Daimlers and Guys. On the right is no.108, a 1968 Leyland Panther PSUR1A/1R with Strachans 47-seat two-door bodywork, one of a batch of 24. Sunderland famously went for flat fare operation and the use of tokens in the mid-1960s, and bought a varied fleet of buses to operate its services. As well as Panthers there were Panther Cubs, AEC Swifts, Bristol RELLs and Daimler Roadliners, most with similarly-styled bodywork built by Marshall and Metro-Cammell as well as Strachans.
Geoff Lumb

Sunderland Corporation also bought Daimler Fleetlines with distinctively-styled Roe bodies at the time municipal operators were seeking to make the bodywork on rear-engined double-deckers more attractive.
Geoff Lumb

Above: Gillett Bros standardised on AEC Reliances for its bus fleet.
This 36ft example has Plaxton Derwent 51-seat bodywork.
G Coxon

Below: Photographed at OK's Bishop Auckland garage in April
1970, a new addition to the mixed fleet, a former Brighton Hove
& District 1954 Bristol KSW6G with 60-seat ECW body.
G E Hutchinson

Above: General Omnibus Services operated in the Chester-le-Street area, usually with Duple-bodied Bedfords, but this was an early Plaxton-bodied bus, a 1957 AEC Reliance with a style of body that predated the Highway design that would become familiar with independents in the north-east.
Photobus

Below: Gypsy Queen provided the service between Durham and Langley Mill, typically with Duple-bodied Bedford SBs like WPT 950 seen here.
Photobus

Sunderland Corporation was absorbed into Tyneside PTE in 1973, in anticipation of the local government reorganisation of 1974 that created Tyne & Wear PTE. One of its distinctive Daimler Fleetlines with Roe bodywork incorporating an unusual flat driver's screen, pulls out of Sunderland's Park Lane bus station.
Mark Page

South Shields Transport Department disappeared into the new Tyneside PTE in 1970, even though it had no through services linking with Newcastle. Looking unusual in PTE yellow/cream is no.379, one of a batch of 18 Daimler CCG6 with Roe 63-seat bodies bought by South Shields in 1964.
Geoff Lumb

Hartlepool no.94, a 1953 Daimler CVG6 with 58-seat Roe body, was still in the fleet in 1970. After 1965 West Hartlepool, as it still was, turned to dual-door single-deckers, building up a large fleet of ECW-bodied Bristol RELL6Ls between 1967 and 1975. The Hartlepool and West Hartlepool undertakings were combined in April 1967.

Charles Dean/Kevin Lane collection

Above left: Before it turned to Bristol RELL6Ls, West Hartlepool bought Leyland Leopard L1s including five with 42-seat dual-door ECW bodies, like Hartlepool no.34 seen here. These were early examples of ECW bodies for non-Tilling fleets and on Leyland chassis, following the Leyland-Bristol share exchange that brought Bristol and ECW products back on to the open market.
Geoff Lumb

Above right: Darlington Corporation was another north-east municipal operator that moved from traditional front-engined double-deckers to rear-engined single-deckers. An example of the old guard is this 1957 Guy Arab IV with Roe 61-seat bodywork, seen in the town centre.
Geoff Lumb

Left: New to Darlington in 1970, a Daimler Fleetline SRG6LX with 48-seat dual-door Marshall body.
Geoff Lumb

G R Anderson and E W Wilson traded as Economic Bus Service, sharing operation of two routes linking South Shields and Sunderland. This 1963 AEC Reliance with 36ft Plaxton body carries fleetnumber 6.
Charles Dean/Kevin Lane collection

Above: Plaxton Highway bodywork fitted to a more unusual chassis, an Albion Aberdonian, essentially a lighter-weight Leyland Tiger Cub. It is in the fleet of the Consett area independent, Armstrongs of Ebchester.
Photobus

Below: One of six Leyland Atlantean PDR1/3 with Roe 75-seat bodies bought in 1968 by Tees-side Railless Traction Board but delivered in the turquoise livery of the newly-created Teesside Municipal Transport, which was set up that year. It is seen at the Roe coachworks in Leeds prior to delivery.
Roe

Above: Another new bus delivered in the Teesside turquoise/cream livery was this 1967 Stockton Corporation Leyland Panther Cub PSURC1/1 with 43-seat Park Royal body, similar to contemporary Manchester Corporation deliveries.
Park Royal

Below: In Teesside turquoise but still wearing Stockton Corporation fleetnames, a 1964 Leyland Atlantean PDR1/1 with Park Royal 74-seat body; similar bodywork was supplied on London Transport's experimental batches of Atlanteans and Daimler Fleetlines.
Photobus

Above: A later Economic AEC Reliance/Plaxton carries the Anderson's name on the front, at Sunderland.
Geoff Lumb

Below: Gillett Bros of Quarrington Hill operated a well turned-out fleet, mainly AECs with Plaxton bodywork, like this 1970 Reliance/Highway seen in Bishop Auckland. The company was taken over by United Auto in 1974.
Geoff Lumb

Above: Best-known and possibly best-loved of the County Durham independents was OK Motor Services of Bishop Auckland, with a 1970 fleet of 36 buses, including this impressive 1958 Leyland Titan PD3/6 with 73-seat Roe body, seen in Bishop Auckland.
Mark Page

Below: Bond Bros, Willington, operated into Bishop Auckland from its home village. This is a 1966 AEC Reliance with Plaxton Highway bodywork, seen in Bishop Auckland.
Mark Page

Above: New deliveries to Teesside in 1970 were 15 of these Leyland Atlantean PDR1A/1R with dual-door Northern Counties 71-seat bodies.
Photobus

Below: Newly repainted into an early version of the Teesside Transport livery, a 1967 former Teesside Railless Traction Board Leyland Titan PD2A/27 with Roe 61-seat body.
Photobus

Above: A Middlesbrough Corporation contribution to the new Teesside Municipal Transport fleet, a 1965 Daimler Fleetline CRG6LW with 70-seat Northern Counties body, one of a large fleet of similar buses incorporated into the initial Teesside fleet. The undertaking would go on to buy many more Northern Counties Fleetlines in the early 1970s.

Photobus

Below: One of the older buses that passed into the new Teesside fleet in 1968, a former Stockton Corporation 1960 Leyland Titan PD2/40 with Weymann 63-seat body, seen here in Stockton High Street.

Photobus/T Sykes/OTA

Above: **Teesside Municipal Transport operated the UK's penultimate trolleybus system in the industrial area east of Middlesbrough. It closed in April 1971 and at South Bank depot in its last days is no.T282, a 1950 Sunbeam F4 with a 1963 Roe 61-seat body, new to the Tees-side Railless Traction Board.**
Charles Dean/Kevin Lane collection

Below: **Wearing the unusual turquoise livery adopted by Teesside Municipal Transport, a former Stockton Corporation 1955 Northern Counties-bodied Leyland Titan PD2/12 in Middlesbrough.**
Charles Dean/Kevin Lane collection